Clothed in Strength and Dignity

Lisa Jennings
1 Peter 3:4

Written & Illustrated
by Lisa Jennings

and she laughs without fear of the future

CHERISHING & COLORING THROUGH PROVERBS

Clothed in Strength & Dignity:
Cherishing & Coloring Through Proverbs

© 2022 by Lisa Jennings
Wood Village, Oregon

lisathompsonjennings@gmail.com

All rights reserved.

Published in the United State of America

Scripture quotations marked TPT are from The Passion Translation®. Copyright © 2017, 2018 by Passion & Fire Ministries, Inc. Used by permission. All rights reserved. ThePassionTranslation.com.

Scripture quotations are from the ESV® Bible (The Holy Bible, English Standard Version®), copyright © 2001 by Crossway, a publishing ministry of Good News Publishers. Used by permission. All rights reserved.

Scripture quotations marked (NIV) are taken from the Holy Bible, New International Version®, NIV®. Copyright © 1973, 1978, 1984, 2011 by Biblica, Inc.™ Used by permission of Zondervan. All rights reserved worldwide. www.zondervan.com. The "NIV" and "New International Version" are trademarks registered in the United States Patent and Trademark Office by Biblica, Inc.™

Scripture quotations marked (AMP) are taken from the Amplified Bible, Copyright © 1954, 1958, 1962, 1964, 1965, 1987 by The Lockman Foundation. Used by permission.

Scripture quotations taken from the Amplified® Bible (AMPC), Copyright © 1954, 1958, 1962, 1964, 1965, 1987 by The Lockman Foundation. Used by permission. www.lockman.org

NKJV. Scripture taken from the New King James Version®. Copyright © 1982 by Thomas Nelson. Used by permission. All rights reserved.

Scripture quotations marked (NLT) are taken from the Holy Bible, New Living Translation, copyright ©1996, 2004, 2015 by Tyndale House Foundation. Used by permission of Tyndale House Publishers, Carol Stream, Illinois 60188. All rights reserved.

Scripture quotations taken from the (NASB®) New American Standard Bible®, Copyright © 1960, 1971, 1977, 1995, 2020 by The Lockman Foundation. Used by permission. All rights reserved. www.lockman.org

Scripture quotations marked (BBE) are from the Bible in Basic English. Public Domain.

Acknowledgements

My heart is unquestionably full of gratitude not only to God from whom all blessings flow, but also to all my beautiful family and friends He has put into my life who have loved me back to wholeness.

My husband Kevin for showing me love in the most difficult seasons. Your love for me has allowed me to soar on the winds of your encouragement and constant grace.

My sons for their love and forgiveness that has inspired me to want to do great things. Being loved by them has healed my heart. Special thanks to Derek for his assistance with the front cover.

My gracious friend and graphic designer Stacie Butler whose skillful artist heart full of God spoke inspiration to my soul. My wise friend editor Linda Dodge whose love for God's Word cultivated my ideas with great insight and discernment. This talented dynamic duo full of the Holy Spirit have been such a gift to me. I honor their amazing gifting and generosity.

May you be blessed by the inspiration of many and God's undeniable love for you. He is longing to address every hurt, injustice and loss that has impacted your life, thus redressing you in His glorious freedom and redemption.

You have turned my mourning into joyful dancing.
You have taken away my clothes of mourning and clothed me with joy.
Psalm 30:11 NLT

Clothed
in Strength and Dignity

Cherishing & Coloring Through Proverbs

Written & Illustrated by Lisa Jennings

Therefore, as God's chosen people, holy and dearly loved,
clothed yourself with compassion, kindness,
humility, gentleness, and patience.
Colossians. 3:12 NIV

Hello, Beautiful!

Listen,
my dearest
darling,
you are
so beautiful—
you are
beauty itself
to me!

*Song of Songs
4:1 TPT*

...let the adorning be
the hidden person of the heart
with the imperishable beauty
of a gentle and quiet spirit,
which in God's sight is very precious.
1 Peter 3:4 ESV

The Journal's Inspiration

Welcome! I'm so happy this journal is in your hands and cannot wait to have you experience the goodness of God as you journal through the book of Proverbs.

The Clothed in Strength & Dignity Journal was created not only from my love for journaling and occasional doodling but also from a longing to create a devotional book after watching the movie 27 Dresses. Though this concept may not sound spiritual, that next day after I watched the movie, I felt inspired to draw 27 little dresses in my journal, redeeming the truth nuggets revealed to me. Each new day I read one chapter in the book of Proverbs as I searched for daily wisdom, choosing one verse to ponder, writing it down, and titling my dress.

Truth be told, I was not a fan of all of the aspects of the movie's content, yet watching the main character Jane's strong desire to please people struck a chord in me. For I, too, have lost my identity in the process of trying to please people throughout my life. Jane somehow found herself saying yes to being a bridesmaid 27 times with an underlining hope that one day these brides would return the favor. Not only that, but Jane's sentimentality lured her to cram every one of those 27 bridesmaid dresses into her closet, leaving no room in her closet or life to spread her God given wings and fly.

For me, people-pleasing became a counterfeit love that was based on fear of rejection, crowding out God's perfect love that casts out all fear, as 1 John 4:18 promises.

Eventually Jane found her true love and cleaned out her closet, for in that true love was revealed the truth she needed—spurring her to embrace the positive changes that were necessary for her newfound freedom. God's love will do that for us and so much more. One touch from God will transform your life forever. Accepting Him as your Lord and Savior and choosing to follow Him every day will be the best decision you will ever make.

When Jane married the man of her dreams, those 27 brides became her bridesmaids, returning the favor just as she hoped they would do.

May you find God's love for you in fresh new ways; may your personal journey of being clothed in strength and dignity allow you to more fully experience laughter without fear of the future.

Enjoy!

Lisa Jennings

Clothe yourself in...

compassion

kindness

humility

gentleness

Therefore, as God's chosen people,
holy and dearly loved,
clothed yourself with
compassion, kindness, humility, gentleness, and patience.
Colossians 3:12 NIV

Journal Instructions

♥ The journal progresses through the book of Proverbs from Chapter 1 to Chapter 31.

♥ **One dress to color and one highlighted verse each day.** The selected verse to ponder correlates with that chapter.

♥ **Hanging with Jesus!** The page opposite the dress and verse for that day will have a few questions about the highlighted verse and a place to write your Garment of Praise—your gratitude to God or something for which you are thankful.

♥ **Devotions.** If you choose to read the whole chapter (which I encourage) you may use this space for your thoughts or study notes.

♥ **Doodle or Dream.** Use your own quiet time style with Jesus that will promote personal growth and intimacy with Him.

♥ Blank pages at the end the journal may be used to create a collage of words or phrases, or sketch or draw, to help you reflect on your learning and or new awareness of God or yourself that emerged as you worked through each chapter.

♥ I have used The Passion Translation of the Bible frequently because of the poetic way it is written. I have felt God's love in a deeper level through incorporating this translation. Feel free to use any Bible translation with which you are comfortable.

The beautiful bouquet of God's Wisdom

The Book of Proverbs is a beautiful bouquet of God's wisdom and revelation knowledge. Mainly written by King Solomon, this book stands poised and ready for us to daily gather up its fragrant truths in the 31 chapters it provides the reader. Wisdom is poetically woven throughout the pages, giving us answers to our human condition through the lens of God's divine solutions. Once we apply the wisdom of the aromatic truths to our lives, we cannot help but spread that scent wherever we go as our lives reflect the image of God more fully and completely.

Our lives are a Christ-like fragrance rising up to God.
2 Corinthians 2:15 NLT

Adorned with Grace

grace filled

Pay close attention, my child, to your father's wise words
and never forget your mother's instructions.
For their insight will bring you success,
adorning you with grace-filled thoughts
and giving you reins to guide your decisions.
Proverbs 1: 8-9 TPT

Hanging with Jesus

♥ Reflect on a parent, grandparent teacher, relative, neighbor, or other adult that impacted your life as a child or teen. What did they say or do that felt affirming or encouraging? How did that person "adorn you with grace"?

♥ Do you feel adorned with grace? Why or why not?

♥ What are you thankful for today?

- Your gratitude may be a simple word or phrase, a person, an experience, or something that God "whispers" to you from the pages of His book (The Bible). Some days maybe all you can do is thank God for breath in your lungs, or that you saw a flower, or that someone said a kinds word to you.

- Words, pictures, rewrite the Proverb for the day, or use whatever form of expression fits you today. *Example: Thank you, Lord, for adorning me with grace-filled thoughts as I go about my day.*

♥ My garment of praise today is ...

Proverbs 1
Doodle or Dream

Adorn yourself with majesty and splendor,
and clothe yourself with honor and glory.
Job 40:10 NIV

Proverbs 1

Devotions

Prompts: What words or phrases or ideas stand out for you as you read and reflect on Proverbs 1? What questions come to mind relationships, or yourself? What words describe God? What words or ideas indicate how God sees you?

_____

_____

_____

_____

_____

_____

_____

_____

_____

_____

_____

_____

_____

_____

_____

_____

_____

_____

_____

_____

Grace is the beauty of form under the influence of freedom.
~ Friedrich Schiller

Divine Design

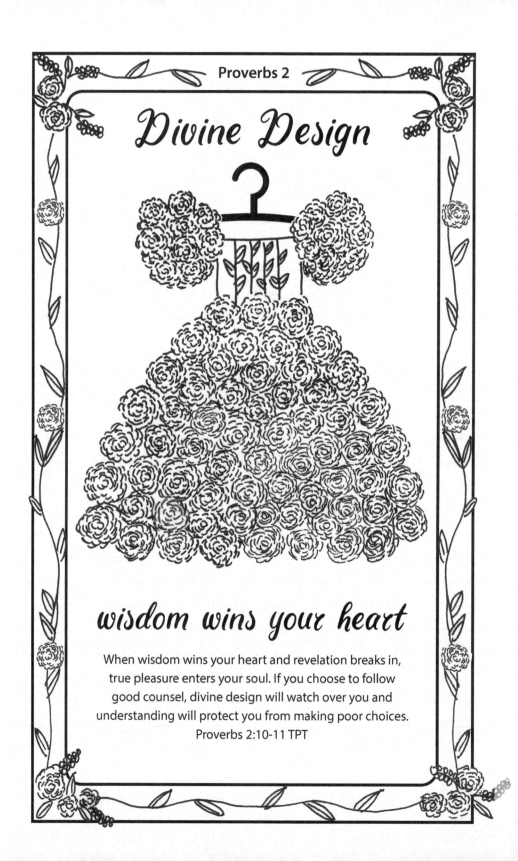

wisdom wins your heart

When wisdom wins your heart and revelation breaks in, true pleasure enters your soul. If you choose to follow good counsel, divine design will watch over you and understanding will protect you from making poor choices.

Proverbs 2:10-11 TPT

Hanging with Jesus

❤ In what area of your heart have you allowed wisdom to break in?

❤ Identify one time when you followed good counsel. Who was involved? What was the situation? How did your choice impact your life?

❤ What is one area of your life where you are contending for understanding and wisdom and moving away from poor choices?

❤ Where can you see God's divine design in yourself or someone you know?

❤ What are you thankful for today?

My garment of praise today is . . .

Proverbs 2
Doodle or Dream

He has made everything beautiful and appropriate in its time.
He has also planted eternity [a sense of divine purpose] in the human heart
[a mysterious longing which nothing under the sun can satisfy, except God]—
yet man cannot find out (comprehend, grasp) what God has done
(His overall plan) from the beginning to the end.
Ecclesiastes 3:11 AMP

Proverbs 2

Devotions

Prompts: What words or phrases or ideas stand out for you as you read and reflect on Proverbs 2? What questions come to mind relationships, or yourself? What words describe God? What words or ideas indicate how God sees you?

_____

_____

_____

_____

_____

_____

_____

_____

_____

_____

_____

_____

_____

_____

_____

_____

_____

_____

_____

_____

The spark of divine dwells in thee: Let it grow.
~ Ella Wheeler Wilcox

Sweet Wisdom

wholeness

The ways of wisdom are sweet,
always drawing you into the place of wholeness.
Proverbs 3:17 TPT

Hanging with Jesus

♥ In what area of your life do you see wholeness that came from wisdom?

♥ Identify a personal situation or relationship that could be improved if you acted on some godly advice or wisdom you have received. What is one step you can take to move forward in doing that?

♥ What are you thankful for today?

My garment of praise today is ...

Proverbs 3
Doodle or Dream

In the same way, wisdom is sweet to your soul.
If you find it, you will have a bright future,
and your hopes will not be cut short.
Proverbs 24:14 NLT

Proverbs 3

Devotions

Prompts: What words or phrases or ideas stand out for you as you read and reflect on Proverbs 3? What questions come to mind relationships, or yourself? What words describe God? What words or ideas indicate how God sees you?

_____

_____

_____

_____

_____

_____

_____

_____

_____

_____

_____

_____

_____

_____

_____

_____

_____

_____

_____

_____

The invariable mark of wisdom is to see the miraculous in the common.
~ Ralph Waldo Emerson

Beauty & Grace

adorned

You will be adorned with beauty and grace,
and wisdom's glory will wrap itself around you,
making you victorious in the race.
Proverbs 4:9 TPT

Hanging with Jesus

♥ Where has wisdom made you victorious recently?

♥ What relationship or situation are you currently facing that can benefit from God's wisdom? Write a short prayer, asking God for his guidance and wisdom.

♥ What are you thankful for today?

My garment of praise today is ...

Proverbs 4
Doodle or Dream

You are altogether beautiful, my darling;
there is no flaw in you.
Song of Solomon. 4:7 NIV

Devotions

Prompts: What words or phrases or ideas stand out for you as you read and reflect on Proverbs 4? What questions come to mind relationships, or yourself? What words describe God? What words or ideas indicate how God sees you?

_____

_____

_____

_____

_____

_____

_____

_____

_____

_____

_____

_____

_____

_____

_____

_____

_____

_____

_____

_____

_____

_____

_____

_____

Never lose an opportunity of seeing anything beautiful,
for beauty is God's handwriting.
~ Ralph Waldo Emerson

Heart

wisdom will enter your heart

Listen carefully to my advice
so that wisdom and discernment will enter your heart,
and then the words you speak will express what you've learned.
Proverbs 5:1-2 TPT

Hanging with Jesus

♥ What is one area of your life where God brought truth and hope where there once was sin?

♥ What are you thankful for today?

My garment of praise today is . . .

Proverbs 5
Doodle or Dream

Let the words of my mouth and the meditation of my heart
be acceptable in your sight,
Oh, Lord, my Rock and my Redeemer.
Psalm 19:14 ESV

Proverbs 5

Devotions

Prompts: What words or phrases or ideas stand out for you as you read and reflect on Proverbs 5? What questions come to mind relationships, or yourself? What words describe God? What words or ideas indicate how God sees you?

_____

_____

_____

_____

_____

_____

_____

_____

_____

_____

_____

_____

_____

_____

_____

_____

_____

_____

_____

_____

_____

There is no charm equal to tenderness of heart.
~ Jane Austen

Truth's Light

shining

For truth is a bright beam of light
shining into every area of your life,
instructing and correcting you to
discover the ways to godly living.
Proverbs 6:23 TPT

Hanging with Jesus

♥ Name one truth that God shined into your life this week. How can that truth lead you deeper into godly living?

♥ What are you thankful for today?

My garment of praise today is ...

Proverbs 6
Doodle or Dream

When Jesus spoke again to the people, he said,
"I am the light of the world. Whoever follows me will never walk in darkness,
but will have the light of life.
John 8:12 NIV

Proverbs 6

Devotions

Prompts: What words or phrases or ideas stand out for you as you read and reflect on Proverbs 6? What questions come to mind relationships, or yourself? What words describe God? What words or ideas indicate how God sees you?

_____

_____

_____

_____

_____

_____

_____

_____

_____

_____

_____

_____

_____

_____

_____

_____

_____

_____

_____

_____

_____

Truth is so rare that it is delightful to tell it.
~ Emily Dickinson

Cherish

cherish my instructions

Treasure my instructions, and cherish them within your heart.
Say to wisdom, "I love you," and to understanding,
"You're my sweetheart."
Proverbs 7 :3-4 TPT

Hanging with Jesus

❤ Think of something you cherish. Maybe this is a person, memory activity or event, or momento. Why is it special—why do you cherish it?

❤ What are the similarities and differences between cherishing God and something else in your life?

❤ How will you choose to cherish God's instruction today?

❤ What are you thankful for today?

My garment of praise today is . . .

Proverbs 7
Doodle or Dream

So let us know and become personally acquainted with Him;
let us press on to know and understand fully the [greatness of the] Lord
[to honor, heed, and deeply cherish Him].
His appearing is prepared and is as certain as the dawn,
And He will come to us [in salvation] like the [heavy] rain,
Like the spring rain watering the earth.
Hosea 6:3 AMP

Proverbs 7

Devotions

Prompts: What words or phrases or ideas stand out for you as you read and reflect on Proverbs 7? What questions come to mind relationships, or yourself? What words describe God? What words or ideas indicate how God sees you?

_____

_____

_____

_____

_____

_____

_____

_____

_____

_____

_____

_____

_____

_____

_____

_____

_____

_____

_____

_____

_____

_____

_____

Friends . . .they cherish one another's hopes.
They are kind to one another's dreams. "
~ Henry David Thoreau

Delight

growing in delight

For the fountain of life pours into you
every time that you find me,
and this is the secret of growing in the delight
and the favor of the Lord.
Proverbs 8:35 TPT

Hanging with Jesus

♥ Where have you found Jesus recently?

♥ What are you thankful for today?

My garment of praise today is ...

Proverbs 8
Doodle or Dream

Delight yourself in the Lord,
and he will give you the desires of your heart.
Psalm 37:4 ESV

Proverbs 8

Devotions

Prompts: What words or phrases or ideas stand out for you as you read and reflect on Proverbs 8? What questions come to mind relationships, or yourself? What words describe God? What words or ideas indicate how God sees you?

_____

_____

_____

_____

_____

_____

_____

_____

_____

_____

_____

_____

_____

_____

_____

_____

_____

_____

_____

_____

Birds sing after a storm; why shouldn't people feel as free
to delight in whatever sunlight remains to them?
~ Rose Kennedy

Fruitful

every year more fruitful

Wisdom will extend your life,
making every year more fruitful than the one before.
Proverbs 9:11 TPT

Hanging with Jesus

♥ What fruit are you seeing in your life right now?

♥ What are you thankful for today?

My garment of praise today is . . .

Proverbs 9
Doodle or Dream

That you might walk worthy of the Lord unto all pleasing,
being fruitful in every good work, and increasing in the knowledge of God.
Colossians 1:10 NKJV

Proverbs 9

Devotions

Prompts: What words or phrases or ideas stand out for you as you read and reflect on Proverbs 9? What questions come to mind relationships, or yourself? What words describe God? What words or ideas indicate how God sees you?

_____

_____

_____

_____

_____

_____

_____

_____

_____

_____

_____

_____

_____

_____

_____

_____

_____

_____

_____

_____

_____

_____

Mountaintops are for views and inspiration, but fruit is grown in the valleys.
~ Billy Graham

God's Ways

are a beautiful resting place

The beautiful ways of God are a safe resting place
for those who have integrity.
Proverbs 10:29 TPT

Hanging with Jesus

♥ How do you define integrity?

♥ How has your integrity brought you into a safe resting place?

♥ Do you need to have a conversation with God about your integrity—maybe identifying a behavior to change or work on, or asking forgiveness? Write out a few thoughts or ideas from your conversation with God about integrity and you.

♥ What are you thankful for today?

My garment of praise today is ...

Proverbs 10
Doodle or Dream

"This is my resting place forever," he said.
"I will live here, for this is the home I desired.
Psalm 132:14 NIV

Devotions

Prompts: What words or phrases or ideas stand out for you as you read and reflect on Proverbs 10? What questions come to mind relationships, or yourself? What words describe God? What words or ideas indicate how God sees you?

_____

_____

_____

_____

_____

_____

_____

_____

_____

_____

_____

_____

_____

_____

_____

_____

_____

_____

_____

_____

_____

The man who has made God his dwelling place
will always have a safe habitation.
~Aiden Wilson Tozer

Blessings

rests on the righteous

The blessing that rests on the righteous
releases strength and favor to the entire city...
Proverbs 11:10 TPT

Hanging with Jesus

♥ Where have God's blessings released strength and favor in your city/ community?

♥ What are you thankful for today?

My garment of praise today is . . .

Proverbs 11
Doodle or Dream

But blessed is the one who trusts in the Lord, whose confidence is in him.
They will be like a tree planted by the water that sends out its roots
by the stream. It does not fear when heat comes its leaves are always green.
It has no worries in a year of drought and never fails to bear fruit.
Jeremiah 17:7-8 NIV

Devotions

Prompts: What words or phrases or ideas stand out for you as you read and reflect on Proverbs 11? What questions come to mind relationships, or yourself? What words describe God? What words or ideas indicate how God sees you?

_____

_____

_____

_____

_____

_____

_____

_____

_____

_____

_____

_____

_____

_____

_____

_____

_____

_____

_____

_____

_____

Reflect upon your present blessings—of which every man has many—
not on your past misfortunes, of which all men have some.
~ Charles Dickens

Peace

joy

. . . those who plan for peace are filled with joy.
Proverbs 12:20 TPT

Hanging with Jesus

♥ How do you plan for peace as you prepare for each day?

♥ What are you thankful for today?

My garment of praise today is ...

Proverbs 12
Doodle or Dream

May the God of hope fill you with all joy and peace in believing,
so that by the power of the Holy Spirit you may abound in hope.
Romans 15:13 ESV

Proverbs 12

Devotions

Prompts: What words or phrases or ideas stand out for you as you read and reflect on Proverbs 12? What questions come to mind relationships, or yourself? What words describe God? What words or ideas indicate how God sees you?

_____

_____

_____

_____

_____

_____

_____

_____

_____

_____

_____

_____

_____

_____

_____

_____

_____

_____

_____

_____

_____

_____

We are not at peace with others because we are not at peace with ourselves, and we are not at peace with ourselves because we are not at peace with God.
~Thomas Merton

Dreams

come true

When hope's dream seems to drag on and on,
the delay can be depressing.
But when at last your dream comes true,
life's sweetness will satisfy your soul.
Proverbs 13:12 TPT

Hanging with Jesus

♥ What God-given dream have you identified for yourself?

♥ Are you experiencing delay in your God-given dream being fulfilled? What hope are you finding in God's promises while you wait?

♥ What are you thankful for today?

My garment of praise today is . . .

Proverbs 13
Doodle or Dream

And afterward, I will pour out my Spirit on all people. Your sons
and daughters will prophesy, your old men will dream dreams,
your young men will see visions.
Joel 2:28 NIV

Proverbs 13

Devotions

Prompts: What words or phrases or ideas stand out for you as you read and reflect on Proverbs 13? What questions come to mind relationships, or yourself? What words describe God? What words or ideas indicate how God sees you?

_____

_____

_____

_____

_____

_____

_____

_____

_____

_____

_____

_____

_____

_____

_____

_____

_____

_____

_____

You are never too old to set another goal or to dream a new dream.
~ C.S Lewis

Confidence

and strength

Confidence and strength flood the hearts of the lovers of God
who live in awe of him,
and their devotion provides their children
with a place of shelter and security.
Proverbs 14:26 TPT

Hanging with Jesus

♥ What is one thing you are in awe of God for today?

♥ If you consider yourself a lover of God, how your confidence and strength changed as a result of that relationship?

♥ What are you thankful for today?

My garment of praise today is ...

Proverbs 14
Doodle or Dream

Though an army besiege me, my heart will not fear,
though war break out against me, even then I will be confident.
Psalms 27:3 NIV

Proverbs 14

Devotions

Prompts: What words or phrases or ideas stand out for you as you read and reflect on Proverbs 14? What questions come to mind relationships, or yourself? What words describe God? What words or ideas indicate how God sees you?

_____

_____

_____

_____

_____

_____

_____

_____

_____

_____

_____

_____

_____

_____

_____

_____

_____

_____

_____

_____

_____

If one advances confidently in the direction of his dreams,
and endeavors to live the life which he has imagined, he will meet
with a success unexpected in common hours.
~ Henry David Thoreau

Cheerful

brings joy

Everything seems to go wrong
when you feel weak and depressed.
But when you choose to be cheerful,
every day will bring you more and more joy and fullness.
Proverbs 15:15 TPT

Hanging with Jesus

♥ Choose two things to be cheerful about today.

♥ What are you thankful for today?

My garment of praise today is . . .

Doodle or Dream

A glad heart makes a cheerful face,
but by sorrow of heart the spirit is crushed.
Proverbs 15:13 ESV

Proverbs 15

Devotions

Prompts: What words or phrases or ideas stand out for you as you read and reflect on Proverbs 15? What questions come to mind relationships, or yourself? What words describe God? What words or ideas indicate how God sees you?

_____

_____

_____

_____

_____

_____

_____

_____

_____

_____

_____

_____

_____

_____

_____

_____

_____

_____

_____

_____

Cheerfulness and contentment are great beautifiers
and are famous preservers of youthful looks.
~ Charles Dickens

Winsome

wisdom

Winsome words pour from a heart of wisdom,
adding value to all you teach.
Nothing is more appealing
than speaking beautiful, life-giving words.
For they release sweetness to our souls
and inner healing to our spirits.
Proverbs 16 : 23-24 TPT

Hanging with Jesus

♥ Ask Holy Spirit to give you living giving words to pour into someone's life today.

♥ What are you thankful for today?

My garment of praise today is ...

Proverbs 16
Doodle or Dream

Let your speech at all times be gracious (pleasant and winsome),
seasoned [as it were] with salt, [so that you may never be at a loss]
to know how you ought to answer anyone
[who puts a question to you].
Colossians 4:6-7 AMPC

Proverbs 16

Devotions

Prompts: What words or phrases or ideas stand out for you as you read and reflect on Proverbs 16? What questions come to mind relationships, or yourself? What words describe God? What words or ideas indicate how God sees you?

_____

_____

_____

_____

_____

_____

_____

_____

_____

_____

_____

_____

_____

_____

_____

_____

_____

_____

_____

_____

Let your life yield a sweet, winsome melody
that this old world needs so desperately. Yes you can if you will.
~ Charles R. Swindoll

Joyful

cheerful heart

A joyful, cheerful heart brings healing to both body and soul.
But the one whose heart is crushed
struggles with sickness and depression.
Proverbs 17 :22 TPT

Hanging with Jesus

♥ Is your heart feeling crushed or joyful today? What do you think is behind your feelings?

♥ The Lord is near to the brokenhearted and saves the crushed in spirit. (Psalm 34:18 ESV). If your heart is crushed, how can you allow the God of all comforts to embrace you with His love?

♥ What are you thankful for today?

My garment of praise today is . . .

Proverbs 17
Doodle or Dream

Be joyful in hope, patient in affliction, faithful in prayer.
Romans 12:12 NIV

Devotions

Prompts: What words or phrases or ideas stand out for you as you read and reflect on Proverbs 17? What questions come to mind relationships, or yourself? What words describe God? What words or ideas indicate how God sees you?

_____

_____

_____

_____

_____

_____

_____

_____

_____

_____

_____

_____

_____

_____

_____

_____

_____

_____

_____

_____

_____

A joyful heart is the normal result of a heart burning with love.
She gives most who gives with joy."
~ Mother Teresa

Wisdom

bubbling up

Words of wisdom are like a fresh, flowing brook—
like deep waters that spring forth from within,
bubbling up inside the one with understanding.
Proverbs 18:4 TPT

Hanging with Jesus

♥ What words of wisdom have bubbled up inside of you this week?

♥ What are you thankful for today?

My garment of praise today is ...

Proverbs 18
Doodle or Dream

But the wisdom from above is first pure,
then peaceable, gentle, open to reason,
full of mercy, and good fruits, impartial and sincere.
.James 3:17 ESV

Proverbs 18

Devotions

Prompts: What words or phrases or ideas stand out for you as you read and reflect on Proverbs 18? What questions come to mind relationships, or yourself? What words describe God? What words or ideas indicate how God sees you?

_____

_____

_____

_____

_____

_____

_____

_____

_____

_____

_____

_____

_____

_____

_____

_____

_____

_____

_____

_____

Turn your wounds into wisdom.
~ Oprah Winfrey

Hanging with Jesus

♥ Take a minute to ask the Holy Spirit to reveal His knowledge to you today. Write down any words or pictures that come to mind.

♥ What are you thankful for today?

My garment of praise today is ...

Proverbs 19
Doodle or Dream

That the God of our Lord Jesus Christ, the Father of glory, may give you
a spirit of wisdom and of revelation in the knowledge of him,
Ephesians 1:17 ESV

Proverbs 19

Devotions

Prompts: What words or phrases or ideas stand out for you as you read and reflect on Proverbs 19? What questions come to mind relationships, or yourself? What words describe God? What words or ideas indicate how God sees you?

_____

_____

_____

_____

_____

_____

_____

_____

_____

_____

_____

_____

_____

_____

_____

_____

_____

_____

_____

_____

_____

_____

Jesus, on the cross set us free. We should make ourselves free
by walking in the revelation of this knowledge.
~J.K. Bentil

Lovers of God have been given
eyes to see and ears to hear from God.
Proverbs 20:12 TPT

Hanging with Jesus

♥   What have you seen and heard this week that was given to you by God?

♥   What are you thankful for today?

My garment of praise today is . . .

Proverbs 20
Doodle or Dream

And the Lord direct your hearts into the love of God,
and into the patient waiting for Christ.
2 Thessalonians 3:5 ESV

Proverbs 20

Devotions

Prompts: What words or phrases or ideas stand out for you as you read and reflect on Proverbs 20? What questions come to mind relationships, or yourself? What words describe God? What words or ideas indicate how God sees you?

_____

_____

_____

_____

_____

_____

_____

_____

_____

_____

_____

_____

_____

_____

_____

_____

_____

_____

_____

_____

No matter what storm you face, you need to know that God loves you.
He has not abandoned you.
~ Franklin Graham

Drenched with Favor

overflowing

The lovers of God who chase after righteousness
will find all their dreams come true:
an abundant life drenched with favor
and a fountain that overflows with satisfaction.
Proverbs 21:21 TPT

Hanging with Jesus

♥ What dream came true because you chased after righteousness? Or, what dream do you still contend for as you chase after righteousness?

♥ What are you thankful for today?

My garment of praise today is ...

Proverbs 21
Doodle or Dream

For You, O Lord, will bless the righteous;
with favor You will surround him as with a shield.
Psalm 5:12 NKJV

Proverbs 21

Devotions

Prompts: What words or phrases or ideas stand out for you as you read and reflect on Proverbs 21? What questions come to mind relationships, or yourself? What words describe God? What words or ideas indicate how God sees you?

_____

_____

_____

_____

_____

_____

_____

_____

_____

_____

_____

_____

_____

_____

_____

_____

_____

_____

_____

_____

_____

Humility is the gateway into the grace and the favor of God.
~ Harold J. Warner

Surrender

so in love with you

brings life

Laying your life down in tender surrender before the Lord
will bring life, prosperity, and honor as your reward.
Proverbs 22:4 TPT

Hanging with Jesus

♥ What do you need to surrender to the Lord? This might involve relationship, finances, a job, ministry, marriage and/or family, time, etc.

♥ What are you thankful for today?

My garment of praise today is ...

Proverbs 22
Doodle or Dream

And he said to all, "If anyone would come after me, let him deny himself
and take up his cross daily and follow me.
Luke 9:23 ESV

Proverbs 22

Devotions

Prompts: What words or phrases or ideas stand out for you as you read and reflect on Proverbs 22? What questions come to mind relationships, or yourself? What words describe God? What words or ideas indicate how God sees you?

_____

_____

_____

_____

_____

_____

_____

_____

_____

_____

_____

_____

_____

_____

_____

_____

_____

_____

_____

_____

_____

Tomorrow's freedom is found in today's surrender.
When I let go I live fully alive.
~ Shree Saranam

Living Hope

never fades away

Your future is bright and filled with a living hope
that will never fade away. As you listen to me,
my beloved child, you will grow in wisdom and
your heart will be drawn into understanding,
which will empower you to make right decisions.
Proverbs 23:18-19 TPT

Hanging with Jesus

♥ What words, questions, or responses come to mind when you think about "living hope" and a "bright future"?

♥ Think of a time when wisdom empowered you to make the right decision. What was the situation? What happened?

♥ What are you thankful for today?

My garment of praise today is ...

Doodle or Dream

Blessed be the God and Father of our Lord Jesus Christ!
According to his great mercy, he has caused us to be born again
to a living hope through the resurrection of Jesus Christ from the dead.
1 Peter 1:3 ESV

Proverbs 23

Devotions

Prompts: What words or phrases or ideas stand out for you as you read and reflect on Proverbs 23? What questions come to mind relationships, or yourself? What words describe God? What words or ideas indicate how God sees you?

_____

_____

_____

_____

_____

_____

_____

_____

_____

_____

_____

_____

_____

_____

_____

_____

_____

_____

_____

_____

_____

_____

Let your hopes, not your hurts, shape your future.
~ Robert H. Schuller

Builders

wise people build

Wise people are builders they build families, businesses, communities. And through intelligence and insight their enterprises are established and endure. Because of their skilled leadership, the hearts of people are filled with the treasures of wisdom and the pleasures of spiritual wealth.

Proverbs 24:3-4 TPT

Hanging with Jesus

♥ How does your perspective change about yourself and your choices when you call yourself a builder?

♥ What are you building lately with your God-given wisdom?

♥ What are you thankful for today?

My garment of praise today is ...

Doodle or Dream

And all your builders will be made wise by the Lord;
and great will be the peace of your children.
Isaiah 54:13 BBE

Devotions

Prompts: What words or phrases or ideas stand out for you as you read and reflect on Proverbs 24? What questions come to mind relationships, or yourself? What words describe God? What words or ideas indicate how God sees you?

_____
_____
_____
_____
_____
_____
_____
_____
_____
_____
_____
_____
_____
_____
_____
_____
_____
_____
_____
_____
_____
_____

Friend, there's no greater investment in life than in being a people builder.
Relationships are more important than our accomplishments.
~ Joel Osteen

Trustworthy

messengers refresh the heart

A reliable, trustworthy messenger refreshes the heart
of his master, like a gentle snowfall at harvest time.
Proverbs 25:13 TPT

Hanging with Jesus

♥ Write about a time you were a trustworthy messenger and how you felt about the experience.

♥ What are you thankful for today?

My garment of praise today is . . .

Proverbs 25
Doodle or Dream

It is a trustworthy statement deserving full acceptance.
For it is for this we labor and strive, because we have fixed our hope
on the living God, who is the Savior of all men, especially of believers.
1 Timothy 4:9-10 NASB

Devotions

Prompts: What words or phrases or ideas stand out for you as you read and reflect on Proverbs 25? What questions come to mind relationships, or yourself? What words describe God? What words or ideas indicate how God sees you?

_____

_____

_____

_____

_____

_____

_____

_____

_____

_____

_____

_____

_____

_____

_____

_____

_____

_____

_____

_____

If you want to be trusted, be trustworthy.

~ Stephen Covey

Powerless to Harm

with no place to land

An undeserved curse
will be powerless to harm you.
It may flutter over you like a bird,
but it will find no place to land.
Proverbs 26:2 TPT

Hanging with Jesus

♥ Recall a time an undeserved curse was thrust your way. How did you respond? Did that curse find a place to land in your life, or simply flutter over you? How would you respond now to a similar situation?

♥ What are you thankful for today?

My garment of praise today is …

Proverbs 26
Doodle or Dream

You are of God, little children, and have overcome them,
because He who is in you is greater than he who is in the world.
1 John 4:4 NASB

Proverbs 26
Devotions

Prompts: What words or phrases or ideas stand out for you as you read and reflect on Proverbs 26? What questions come to mind relationships, or yourself? What words describe God? What words or ideas indicate how God sees you?

_____

_____

_____

_____

_____

_____

_____

_____

_____

_____

_____

_____

_____

_____

_____

_____

_____

_____

_____

_____

Evil is powerless if the good are unafraid.
~ Ronald Regan

Friendship

refreshes the soul

Sweet friendships refresh the soul
and awaken our hearts with joy,
for good friends are like the anointing oil
that yields the fragrant incense of God's presence.
Proverbs 27:9 TPT

Hanging with Jesus

♥ Write about a sweet friendship that awakened your heart to joy.

♥ What are you thankful for today?

My garment of praise today is . . .

Proverbs 27
Doodle or Dream

A friend loves at all times, and a brother is born for adversity.
Proverbs 17:17 ESV

Proverbs 27

Devotions

Prompts: What words or phrases or ideas stand out for you as you read and reflect on Proverbs 27? What questions come to mind relationships, or yourself? What words describe God? What words or ideas indicate how God sees you?

_____

_____

_____

_____

_____

_____

_____

_____

_____

_____

_____

_____

_____

_____

_____

_____

_____

_____

_____

_____

_____

_____

Let us be grateful to people who make us happy,
they are the charming gardeners who make our souls blossom.
~ Marcel Proust

Triumphant

joy of God

The triumphant joy of God's lovers
releases great glory. But when
the wicked rise to power,
everyone goes into hiding.
Proverbs 28:12 TPT

Hanging with Jesus

♥ How is your joy releasing glory to those around you?

♥ What are you thankful for today?

My garment of praise today is ...

Doodle or Dream

Now to Him who is able to keep you from stumbling or falling into sin, and to
present you unblemished [blameless and faultless] in the presence
of His glory with triumphant joy and unspeakable delight.
Jude 1:24 AMP

Proverbs 28

Devotions

Prompts: What words or phrases or ideas stand out for you as you read and reflect on Proverbs 28? What questions come to mind relationships, or yourself? What words describe God? What words or ideas indicate how God sees you?

_____

_____

_____

_____

_____

_____

_____

_____

_____

_____

_____

_____

_____

_____

_____

_____

_____

_____

_____

_____

_____

_____

I learned that courage was not the absence of fear, but the triumph over it. The
brave man is not he who does not feel afraid,
but he who conquers that fear.
~ Nelson Mandela

High Places

seated with the Lord

Fear and intimidation is a trap that holds you back.
But when you place your confidence in the Lord,
you will be seated in the high place.
Proverbs 29:25 TPT

Hanging with Jesus

♥ In what area have you recently placed your confidence in the Lord?

♥ What do you think it means to be seated in a high place?

♥ What are you thankful for today?

My garment of praise today is ...

Proverbs 29
Doodle or Dream

He makes my feet like hinds' feet,
And sets me upon my high places.
Psalm 18:33 NASB

Devotions

Prompts: What words or phrases or ideas stand out for you as you read and reflect on Proverbs 29? What questions come to mind relationships, or yourself? What words describe God? What words or ideas indicate how God sees you?

_____

_____

_____

_____

_____

_____

_____

_____

_____

_____

_____

_____

_____

_____

_____

_____

_____

_____

_____

_____

_____

_____

_____

"O Shepherd. You said you would make my feet like hinds' feet and set me upon High Places." "Well", he answered, "the only way to develop hinds' feet is to go by the paths which the hinds use."
~Hannah Hurnard

Faithful

every promise of God

Every promise from the faithful God
is pure and proves to be true.
He is a wraparound shield of protection
for all his lovers who run to hide in him.
Proverbs 30:5 TPT

Hanging with Jesus

♥ Recall a time recently when you felt God's wraparound shield of protection.

♥ What are you thankful for today?

My garment of praise today is . . .

Proverbs 30
Doodle or Dream

Your kingdom is an everlasting kingdom, and your dominion endures
throughout all generations. [The Lord is faithful in all his words
and kind in all his works.] The Lord upholds all who are falling
and raises up all who are bowed down. The eyes of all look to you,
and you give them their food in due season.
Psalm 145:13-15 ESV

Proverbs 30

Devotions

Prompts: What words or phrases or ideas stand out for you as you read and reflect on Proverbs 30? What questions come to mind relationships, or yourself? What words describe God? What words or ideas indicate how God sees you?

_____

_____

_____

_____

_____

_____

_____

_____

_____

_____

_____

_____

_____

_____

_____

_____

_____

_____

_____

_____

_____

_____

God is faithful, and that trumps all our problems, tears, tragedies,
and the very prospect of death itself.
~ David Jeremiah

Hanging with Jesus

♥ When she speaks, her words are wise, and she gives instructions with kindness. She carefully watches everything in her household and suffers nothing from laziness. Her children stand and bless her. Her husband praises her: "There are many virtuous and capable women in the world, but you surpass them all!" Charm is deceptive, and beauty does not last; but a woman who fears the Lord will be greatly praised. Reward her for all she has done. Let her deeds publicly declare her praise. (Proverbs 31: 26-31 NLT)

♥ How does these words reflect a radiant woman? With which words or phrases do you most identify?

♥ What are you thankful for today?

My garment of praise today is ...

Proverbs 31
Doodle or Dream

They looked to Him and were radiant;
Their faces will never blush in shame or confusion.
Psalm 34:5 KJV

Proverbs 31

Devotions

Prompts: What words or phrases or ideas stand out for you as you read and reflect on Proverbs 31? What questions come to mind relationships, or yourself? What words describe God? What words or ideas indicate how God sees you?

_____

_____

_____

_____

_____

_____

_____

_____

_____

_____

_____

_____

_____

_____

_____

_____

_____

_____

_____

_____

Beauty is a radiance that originates from within
and comes from inner security and strong character.
~ Jane Seymour